RUGBY
WORLD CUP™
JAPAN 2019

KIDS'
HANDBOOK

RUGBY
WORLD CUP™
JAPAN 日本 2019

Published in 2019

TM © Rugby World Cup Limited 2015

Produced under licence by Carlton Books Limited,
an imprint of the Carlton Publishing Group,
20 Mortimer Street, London W1T 3JW

Text and design © Carlton Books Limited 2019

Author: Clive Gifford
Design: RockJaw Creative
Consultant: Anthony Hobbs
Illustration p34: Peter Liddiard

A catalogue record for this book is available from the British Library.

ISBN: 978-1-78312-469-5

Printed in Dubai

9 8 7 6 5 4 3 2 1

The publishers would like to thank the following sources for their kind permission to reproduce the pictures in this book. Key: T=top, B=bottom, L=left, R=right, C=centre.

Getty Images: /Shaun Botterill: 6-7; /Gabriel Bouys/AFP: 37T; /Lachlan Cunningham: 17; /Stephane de Sakutin/AFP: 18; /Harry Engels: 26; /Julian Finney: 42B; /Stu Forster: 33, 41B; /Laurence Griffiths: 14, 28; /Julian Herbert: 43B; /Mike Hewitt: 36B; /Tom Jenkins: 13BL; /Mark Kolbe: 41T; /Alex Livesey: 39C; /Stephen McCarthy/Sportsfile/Corbis: 38C; /Koki Nagahama: 38T; /David Rodgers: 13R; /David Rogers/The RFU Collection: 41C; /Mark Runnacles: 1L, 19, 22; /Michael Steele: 32, 39B; /Visionhaus: 1CL, 20, 25, 36T, 43T; /Dave Winter/Icon Sport: 42T

Shutterstock: /DeanHarty: 35

World Rugby via Getty Images: /Steve Bardens: 1CR, 1R, 7BR, 10-11, 11TR, 15, 24, 27, 30, 37C, 38B, 43C; /Richard Heathcote: 1C, 4-5, 8, 12-13, 16, 31, 40B; /Chris Lee: 21, 37B, 39T, 40T, 42C; /Matt Lewis: 11B, 23, 29; /Lintao Zhang: 5T

Every effort has been made to acknowledge correctly and contact the source and/or copyright holder of each picture and Carlton Books Limited apologises for any unintentional errors or omissions that will be corrected in future editions of this book.

CONTENTS

MEET THE TEAMS

Note to readers: the facts and stats in this book are accurate as of 18 March, 2019.

The greatest rugby show on Earth

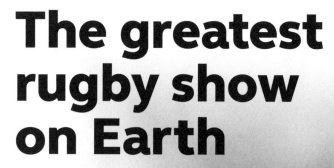

Once every four years, the world's best national rugby union teams gather for Rugby World Cup. This book is the perfect guide to the 2019 tournament, with all the teams, top players, stats, facts and records along with charts to fill in and puzzles to solve.

WHERE IS IT?
The tournament is travelling to Asia for the very first time, where Japan are the hosts. Forty-eight matches will be held at 12 different stadia all around the country.

HOW DOES IT WORK?
Twenty teams are split into four pools of five. Teams in a pool play each other and the top two teams in each pool progress to the quarter-finals. The winners of those matches reach the semi-finals to decide who plays in the final. The losing semi-finalists contest the bronze final.

WHEN IS IT?
The tournament kicks off on 20 September, 2019 when the hosts play Pool A rivals Russia at the Tokyo Stadium. The matches come thick and fast until 2 November, when more than 72,000 fans will watch the final at the International Stadium Yokohama.

WHAT CAN I EXPECT?
Drama, excitement, and a feast of rugby action as different teams, players and tactics clash and challenge each other!

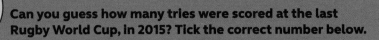

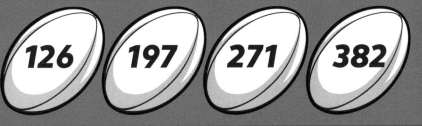

RUGBY WORLD CUP™ JAPAN 2019

TROPHY TOUR トロフィーツアー

Did you know?
The Webb Ellis Cup was made by a London jeweller in 1906, 81 years before the first RWC tournament. Richie McCaw held it aloft in 2015 as New Zealand won Rugby World Cup for a second time in a row. Will they succeed again or will one of the other 19 teams lift the trophy?

Can you guess how many tries were scored at the last Rugby World Cup, in 2015? Tick the correct number below.

126   **197**   **271**   **382**

ABOVE: *Chinese schoolchildren get close to the Webb Ellis Cup on its world tour in 2018.*

LEFT: *Ireland's Robbie Henshaw is tackled by Nicolás Sánchez of Argentina at RWC 2015.*

It's a numbers game

Rugby is all about scoring points and stopping the opposing team from scoring by tackling and defending. There are four ways a team can score points during a match: tries, conversions, penalties and drop goals.

TRIES AND CONVERSIONS

Placing the ball down in the opponent's in-goal area is a try and worth five points. A team that scores a try can add two further points with a conversion kick. This kick is taken from the ground and has to pass between the goalposts to count.

PENALTY KICK

The referee may award a penalty when one team breaks the laws of the game. The opposing team then attempts to kick the ball through the goalposts to score three points. Teams with very accurate goal kickers often win matches.

Did you know?
New Zealand have scored more Rugby World Cup tries than any other nation – 311. They are followed by Australia with 209 and France with 171.

Did you know?
At RWC 2007, Scotland's Chris Paterson kicked every penalty and conversion he attempted – a record 17 out of 17.

ABOVE: *Codie Taylor scores New Zealand's ninth try in their 58-14 win over Namibia at RWC 2015.*

? **Can you match these numbers to the rugby law they apply to?**

15	40	5	10	20	8
Minutes off the pitch for a player who is shown a yellow card	Number of players on each team who form a scrum	Minutes per half	Number worn by a second-row	Players in a team's starting line-up	Additional minutes played when a match goes into extra-time

Here are the top five points scorers at Rugby World Cup. Can you add their names to the table in the correct order?

DAN CARTER		277
MICHAEL LYNAGH		227
GRANT FOX		195
JONNY WILKINSON		191
GAVIN HASTINGS		170

Did you know?
England have scored more drop goals at Rugby World Cup than any other nation – a total of 21.

DROP GOAL
As the match is being played, a player can try to kick the ball from his hands through the posts to score a drop goal worth three points. Jonny Wilkinson famously scored a drop goal to win Rugby World Cup 2003 for England.

RIGHT: Dan Carter kicks a drop goal against South Africa in the semi-final of RWC 2015.

Welcome to Japan

Rugby fans can expect the warmest of welcomes when they arrive in Japan, hosts of Rugby World Cup 2019. There will be fun and games in the fan zones in many cities and appearances by the tournament mascot, Ren-G.

THE BRAVE BLOSSOMS

Japan are known as the Brave Blossoms and play in a distinctive red and white kit. They have suffered some heavy defeats and were the first team to concede 1,000 Rugby World Cup points. However, they also caused arguably the biggest RWC shock of all time by beating South Africa in 2015. Away from Rugby World Cup, they also beat Italy in 2018.

BELOW: Japan celebrate a 26-5 win over Samoa at RWC 2015.

In 2015, Japan became the first team to win three matches but not advance out of their pool. Can you tick the three teams they defeated?

South Africa	Wales	Samoa	Argentina	USA	Fiji	Georgia

RUGBY WORLD CUP 2019 VENUES

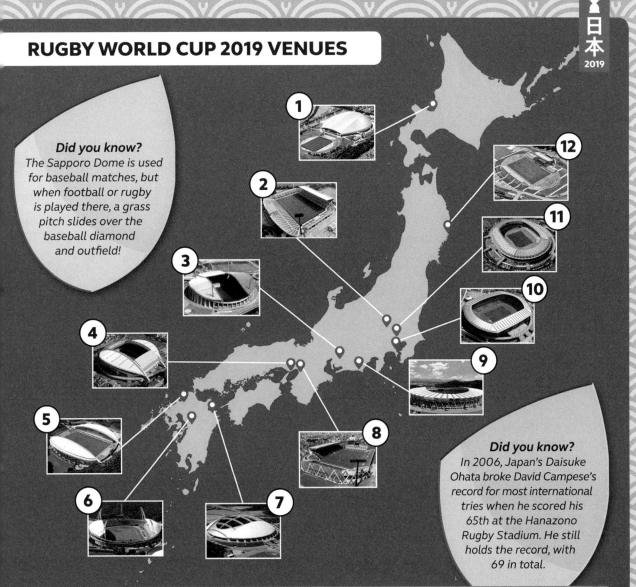

Did you know?
The Sapporo Dome is used for baseball matches, but when football or rugby is played there, a grass pitch slides over the baseball diamond and outfield!

Did you know?
In 2006, Japan's Daisuke Ohata broke David Campese's record for most international tries when he scored his 65th at the Hanazono Rugby Stadium. He still holds the record, with 69 in total.

1. SAPPORO DOME
Completed: 2001
Capacity: 41,410

2. KUMAGAYA RUGBY STADIUM
Completed: 1991
Capacity: 24,000

3. CITY OF TOYOTA STADIUM
Completed: 2001
Capacity: 45,000

4. KOBE MISAKI STADIUM
Completed: 2001
Capacity: 30,132

5. FUKUOKA HAKATANOMORI STADIUM
Completed: 1995
Capacity: 20,049

6. KUMAMOTO STADIUM
Completed: 1998
Capacity: 30,000

7. OITA STADIUM
Completed: 2001
Capacity: 40,000

8. HANAZONO RUGBY STADIUM
Completed: 1929
Capacity: 24,100

9. SHIZUOKA STADIUM ECOPA
Completed: 2001
Capacity: 50,889

10. INTERNATIONAL STADIUM YOKOHAMA
Completed: 1997
Capacity: 72,327

11. TOKYO STADIUM
Completed: 2000
Capacity: 49,970

12. KAMAISHI RECOVERY MEMORIAL STADIUM
Completed: 2018
Capacity: 16,020

Rugby laws

Rugby has lots of laws that have to be followed by the players and are applied by a referee and two assistants. Theirs is a high-pressure job, especially at Rugby World Cup where the stakes are high.

MOVING THE BALL

Players can pass, kick or run with the ball up the pitch to attack the other team's try line. Forward passes are not allowed and if the ball is fumbled or dropped and knocked forward, the other team gets possession. Some players use skilful kicks forward for team-mates to chase, while other players run hard and fast around or through the opponents' defence.

LINEOUTS

If the ball leaves the pitch over the sidelines, the match is usually restarted with a lineout. One player throws the ball down the middle of a corridor formed of two lines of players, one from each team.

YOU'RE THE REF!

Referees have to make dozens of decisions every match. Could you be a referee? Find out by picking the right decision for each of the following match situations.

1) A team kicks off but the ball does not travel forward 10 metres. Do you:
a) Award a penalty
b) Ask the other team whether they want a scrum or to have the kick retaken

2) A player knocks on the ball, hitting it forward deliberately. What do you award?
a) A penalty to the other team
b) A scrum to the other team

3) A team that has been awarded a penalty kicks the ball out along the sidelines. What happens next?
a) A scrum is formed at the point where the kick was taken
b) A lineout occurs with the kicking team given the throw in

CARD SHARP

If a referee spots a player breaking the laws of the game in a serious way, they may show that player a yellow card. The player has to leave the pitch for 10 minutes while his team carry on with one player less. A more serious or dangerous infringement can see a player red-carded and leave the field for the rest of the match.

RIGHT: Romain Poite shows England's Owen Farrell a yellow card at RWC 2015.

LEFT: Scrum-halves such as Wales' Gareth Davies may make 60 or more passes in a match.

Can you guess the total number of red cards awarded to players at the first eight Rugby World Cups?

17   33   48

Did you know?
Three red cards were shown by referee David McHugh in a single RWC match – Canada v South Africa in 1995.

SPOT THE DIFFERENCE
Nigel Owens shows France's Louis Picamoles a yellow card at RWC 2015. Can you spot five differences between the two images?

Champions!

Winning Rugby World Cup is the biggest prize in world rugby. Only four nations have been lucky enough to manage it so far.

1987   2011   2015

NEW ZEALAND

After winning the very first Rugby World Cup in 1987, New Zealand had to wait over 30 years to repeat the feat. In 2011 they overcame France by just one point in the lowest-scoring final ever (8-7), then four years later defeated Australia 34-17 in the highest-scoring final. Can the world number one-ranked team make it three in a row?

RIGHT: New Zealand captain Richie McCaw proudly lifts the Webb Ellis Cup in 2015.

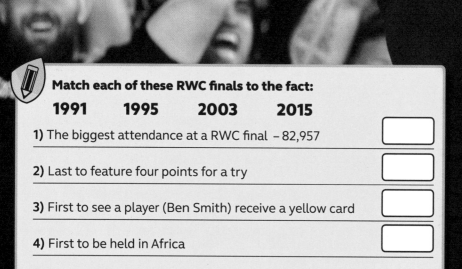

Match each of these RWC finals to the fact:

1991   1995   2003   2015

1) The biggest attendance at a RWC final – 82,957

2) Last to feature four points for a try

3) First to see a player (Ben Smith) receive a yellow card

4) First to be held in Africa

1991   1999

AUSTRALIA

In 1991 Australia became the first team to lift the trophy away from their own continent. Eight years later they set a record for the most points in a final by one team when they defeated France 35-12. They reached the final in 2003 and 2015 but lost both, scoring 17 points on each occasion.

South Africa's Andre Watson is the only referee to have taken charge of two RWC finals. Can you guess which years?

1995   2007

SOUTH AFRICA

The Springboks took advantage of passionate home support in 1995 as they defeated New Zealand in the first final to go to extra-time. In 2007, they contested a try-less final versus England. The tournament's leading points scorer, Percy Montgomery, kicked four penalties to see South Africa triumph again.

ABOVE: *President Nelson Mandela hands the trophy to Francois Pienaar in 1995.*

2003

LEFT: *Jonny Wilkinson kicks the winning drop goal in the 2003 final.*

ENGLAND

After amassing the most points in the tournament of any side (307), England took part in a tense final against hosts Australia in 2003. At 14-14 the match went into extra-time before Jonny Wilkinson kicked a famous last-gasp drop goal to see England home 20-17.

日本 2019

MEET THE TEAMS

IRELAND

First international: **1875**
Previous RWC appearances: **8**
RWC points: **973**
Best finish: **Quarter-finals 1987, 1991, 1995, 2003, 2011, 2015**
Ones to watch: **Johnny Sexton, Conor Murray, Tadhg Furlong, James Ryan, Jacob Stockdale, Keith Earls**

How many Rugby World Cup tries have Ireland scored?

114   **149**   **186**
◯   ◯   ◯

Unscramble the letters to find the names of a current Irish forward and a back.

Achy Alien

☐☐☐☐ ☐☐☐☐☐

Angry Sir Roger

☐☐☐☐☐
☐☐☐☐☐☐☐☐

Did you know?
Ireland have a 100 per cent winning record against 10 of the 16 teams they have faced at Rugby World Cup. They have yet to play a match against England at any of the tournaments.

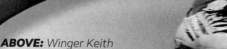

ABOVE: *Winger Keith Earls has already scored eight tries at Rugby World Cup.*

14

POOLA

MEET THE TEAMS
SCOTLAND

First international: **1871**
Previous RWC appearances: **8**
RWC points: **1,142**
Best finish: **Semi-finals 1991**
Ones to watch: **Stuart Hogg, Huw Jones,**
Hamish Watson,
Finn Russell,
Jonny Gray,
John Barclay

LEFT: *Fly-half Finn Russell's vision and passing create many tries for his Scottish team-mates.*

Did you know?
Gavin Hastings once kicked eight penalties in a RWC match against Tonga. He is also the second-highest RWC points scorer, with 227 points.

Match these four Rugby World Cup scores to the teams shown below.

1987: Scotland 20-20

1995: Scotland 89-0

2007: Scotland 56-10

2015: Scotland 34-35

PORTUGAL   **AUSTRALIA**

FRANCE   **IVORY COAST**

MEET THE TEAMS

JAPAN

First international: **1932**
Previous RWC appearances: **8**
RWC points: **526**
Best finish: **Pool stage**
Ones to watch: **Fumiaki Tanaka, Kazuki Himeno, Michael Leitch, Yoshikazu Fujita**

LEFT: *Explosive forward Hendrik Tui has already scored 18 tries for Japan.*

Full-back Ayumu Goromaru is Japan's top all-time international points scorer. Tick the number of points you think he has scored.

- ◯ 148
- ◯ 329
- ◯ 461
- ◯ 572
- ◯ 711
- ◯ 919

Can you match each coach of Japan with the Rugby World Cup they coached the team at?

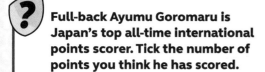

	2003	2011	2015	2019
EDDIE JONES				□
JAMIE JOSEPH				□
SHOGO MUKAI				□
JOHN KIRWAN				□

Did you know?
Before they beat South Africa in the pool stage of RWC 2015, Japan had lost 21 of their 24 matches at Rugby World Cup, drawing two and winning just one.

MEET THE TEAMS

RUSSIA

First international: **1992**
Previous RWC appearances: **1**
RWC points: **57**
Best finish: **Pool stage**
Ones to watch: **Vasily Artemyev,
Vladimir Ostroushko,
Dmitri Gerasimov,
Yuri Kushnarev**

Did you know?
Almost all of the Russian squad play their club rugby in their home country. One exception is the second-row forward Andrei Ostrikov, who has played for English Premiership team Sale Sharks since 2011.

In 2011, Russia scored the most tries by a team making their RWC debut since Samoa in 1991. How many did they score?

◯ **4**   ◯ **6**
◯ **8**   ◯ **10**

RIGHT: *Sharp full-back Vasily Artemyev is Russia's leading try scorer with 30 tries.*

Did you know?
Russia's first international was in 1992 versus the Barbarians team in Moscow. The Russians won 27-23.

MEET THE TEAMS

SAMOA

First international: **1924**
Previous RWC appearances: **7**
RWC points: **654**
Best finish: **Quarter-finals 1991, 1995**
Ones to watch: **Tusi Pisi, TJ Ioane,**
Sinoti Sinoti,
Chris Vui

LEFT: *Playing mostly at fly-half, Tusi Pisi has scored 236 points for Samoa.*

Did you know?
Samoa's biggest win in international rugby was a 115-7 victory over Papua New Guinea in 2009.

? **Which team did Samoa defeat in their very first Rugby World Cup match in 1991?**

◯ **IRELAND**

◯ **WALES**

◯ **FRANCE**

Did you know?
Five brothers – Enele, Alesana, Fereti, Anitelea and Sanele Tuilagi – have all played for Samoa, while a sixth, Manu, plays for England.

MEET THE TEAMS

NEW ZEALAND

First international: **1903**

Previous RWC appearances: **8**

RWC points: **2,302**

Best finish: **Champions 1987, 2011, 2015**

Ones to watch: **Beauden Barrett, Kieran Read, Rieko Ioane, Sam Whitelock, Ben Smith**

Which New Zealand player holds the record for the most RWC wins (20)?

◯ **DAN CARTER**

◯ **RICHIE MCCAW**

◯ **JONAH LOMU**

Against which team did New Zealand record the biggest ever RWC score, a 145-17 victory in 1995?

◯ **PORTUGAL**

◯ **URUGUAY**

◯ **JAPAN**

Did you know?
At Rugby World Cup 1995, Simon Culhane scored 20 conversions and a try for a record 45 points in a match. What's more, it was his debut for the All Blacks!

RIGHT: *With 82 appearances, Aaron Smith is New Zealand's most-capped scrum-half.*

MEET THE TEAMS
SOUTH AFRICA

First international: **1891**
Previous RWC appearances: **6**
RWC points: **1,250**
Best finish: **Champions 1995, 2007**
Ones to watch: **Siya Kolisi, Malcolm Marx,
Willie le Roux,
Duane Vermeulen,
Eben Etzebeth**

**Tick the number of tries
Bryan Habana scored at
Rugby World Cup 2007.**

4   6   8   10
◯   ◯   ◯   ◯

RIGHT: *Powerful prop
Tendai Mtawarira has
played more than 100
times for South Africa.*

*Did you know?
Handré Pollard was
just 21 years old
when he scored
93 points at
RWC 2015.*

*Did you know?
Percy Montgomery's 105
points in 2007 is the
most points scored
by a South African
at a single RWC
tournament.*

**Who did South Africa beat to finish
third at Rugby World Cup 2015?**

◯ **WALES**

◯ **FRANCE**

◯ **ARGENTINA**

MEET THE TEAMS

ITALY

First international: **1929**
Previous RWC appearances: **8**
RWC points: **529**
Best finish: **Pool stage**
Ones to watch: **Sergio Parisse,
Michele Campagnaro,
Matteo Minozzi,
Tommaso Benvenuti**

LEFT: *Tommaso Allan scored 44 points at Rugby World Cup 2015 playing at fly-half.*

? TRUE OR FALSE?

1) Diego Dominguez scored 983 international points for Italy, more than any Australian, South African or Scottish player.

◯ *TRUE* ◯ *FALSE*

2) Italy have won two matches at every single Rugby World Cup except 1999.

◯ *TRUE* ◯ *FALSE*

3) Italy have played more internationals against Romania than any other nation.

◯ *TRUE* ◯ *FALSE*

Did you know?
Sergio Parisse has captained Italy a record 88 times, second in the world only to New Zealand's Richie McCaw.

? Which player appeared in his fifth Rugby World Cup for Italy in 2015?

◯ **SERGIO PARISSE**

◯ **ALESSANDRO TRONCON**

◯ **MAURO BERGAMASCO**

MEET THE TEAMS

NAMIBIA

First international: **1990**
Previous RWC appearances: **5**
RWC points: **214**
Best finish: **Pool stage**
Ones to watch: **Renaldo Bothma,**
　　　　　　　Rohan Kitshoff,
　　　　　　　Chrysander Botha,
　　　　　　　PJ van Lill

LEFT: *Centre JC Greyling has scored 19 tries for Namibia in just 30 matches.*

Can you tick the African nation against which Namibia racked up their biggest international score, an 118-0 win in 2018?

◯ **TUNISIA**

◯ **ZIMBABWE**

◯ **KENYA**

◯ **IVORY COAST**

Did you know?
Namibia have played in every RWC since 1999, but have lost all 19 of their matches.

? **Which of the following is the nickname of the Namibian team?**

◯ **SEA EAGLES**

◯ **WELWITSCHIAS**

◯ **MIGHTY LIONS**

MEET THE TEAMS

CANADA

First international: **1932**

Previous RWC appearances: **8**

RWC points: **527**

Best finish: **Quarter-finals 1991**

Ones to watch: **Phil Mack, Ciaran Hearn, DTH van der Merwe, Djustice Sears-Duru**

LEFT: *Phil Mack breaks through an Italian tackle during a RWC 2015 Pool D match.*

Canada's first international match in 1932 ended in a narrow 9-8 defeat to which side?

○ **JAPAN**

○ **USA**

○ **FRANCE**

Did you know?
In 1999, Canadian fly-half Gareth Rees became the first player to appear at four Rugby World Cups. Twelve years later he became the first Canadian to be inducted into the World Rugby Hall of Fame.

Can you tick two of the teams Canada defeated in the 2018 Repechage tournament in France to qualify for RWC 2019?

○ **GERMANY**

○ **ROMANIA**

○ **BRAZIL**

○ **HONG KONG**

MEET THE TEAMS

ENGLAND

First international: **1871**
Previous RWC appearances: **8**
RWC points: **1,379**
Best finish: **Champions 2003**
Ones to watch: **Jonny May, Owen Farrell, Maro Itoje, Billy Vunipola, Elliot Daly, Mako Vunipola**

Can you unscramble the letters to reveal the name of an England forward and a back?

I Jog Eager Me

☐☐☐☐☐
☐☐☐☐☐☐

Learner Wolf

☐☐☐☐ ☐☐☐☐☐☐☐

England's record RWC win was in 2003 versus Uruguay. What was the score?

○ 57–3

○ 79–9

○ 111–13

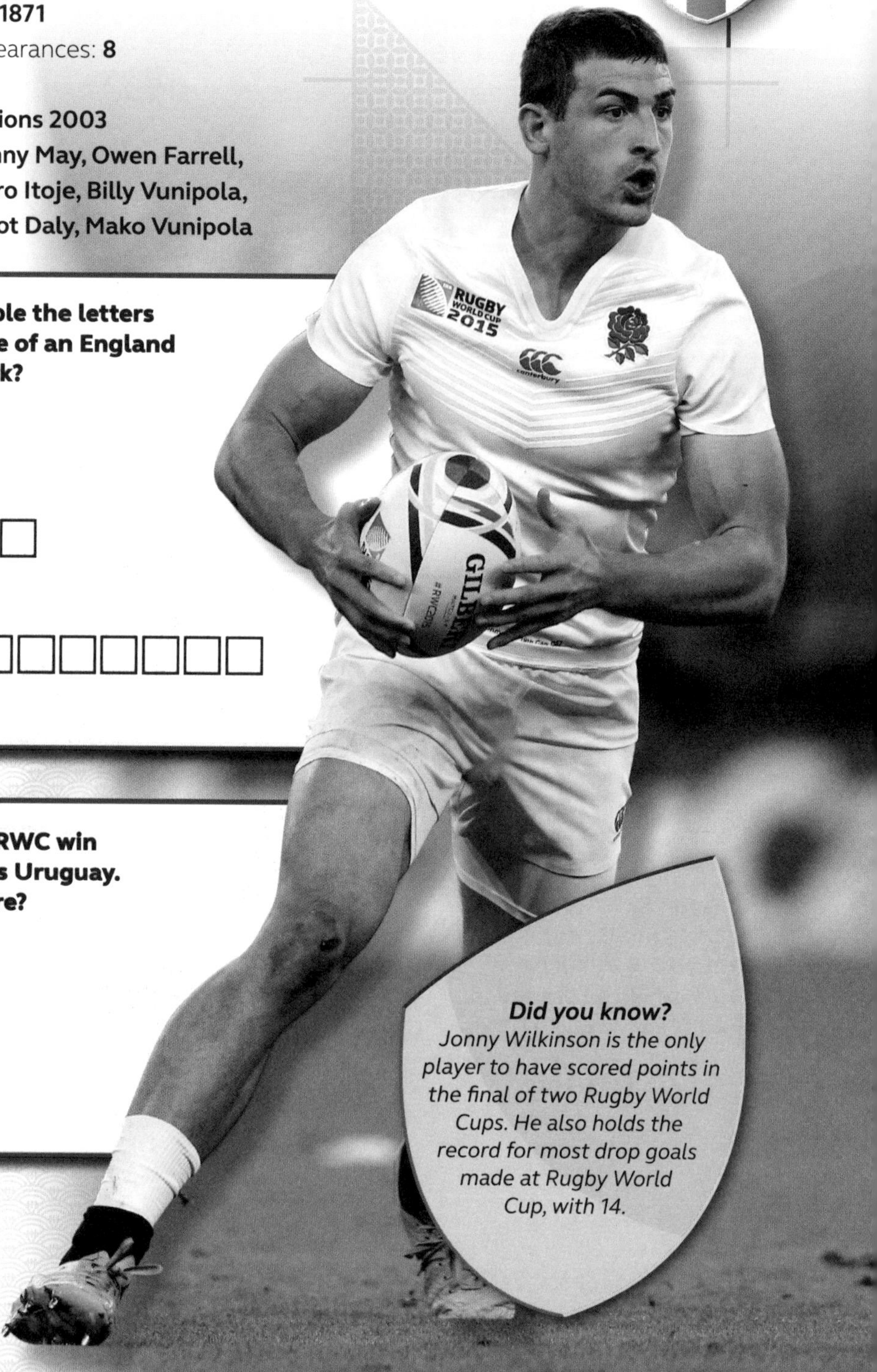

Did you know?
Jonny Wilkinson is the only player to have scored points in the final of two Rugby World Cups. He also holds the record for most drop goals made at Rugby World Cup, with 14.

RIGHT: *Super-speedy winger Jonny May will be aiming to add to his tally of one RWC try.*

MEET THE TEAMS

FRANCE

First international: **1906**
Previous RWC appearances: **8**
RWC points: **1,487**
Best finish: **Runners-up 1987, 1999, 2011**
Ones to watch: **Mathieu Bastareaud, Louis Picamoles, Gaël Fickou, Wesley Fofana, Teddy Thomas, Guilhem Guirado**

? **France will host RWC 2023. Can you tick the two years in which they have hosted or co-hosted the tournament?**

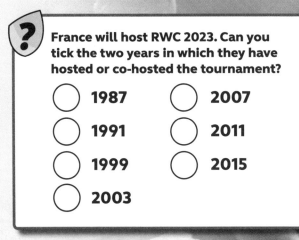

○ **1987**   ○ **2007**

○ **1991**   ○ **2011**

○ **1999**   ○ **2015**

○ **2003**

? **France took part in the first ever draw at Rugby World Cup, in 1987. The score was 20-20, but who were their opponents?**

○ **FIJI**

○ **SCOTLAND**

○ **AUSTRALIA**

○ **ENGLAND**

Did you know?
France are the only northern hemisphere side to make it to at least the quarter-finals of every RWC so far.

RIGHT: *France number eight Louis Picamoles powers through the Irish defence at RWC 2015.*

MEET THE TEAMS

ARGENTINA

First international: **1910**
Previous RWC appearances: **8**
RWC points: **992**
Best finish: **Third place 2007**
Ones to watch: **Agustín Creevy, Nicolás Sánchez, Bautista Delguy, Pablo Matera, Tomás Lavanini**

RIGHT: *Flanker Pablo Matera helped Argentina finish fourth at Rugby World Cup 2015.*

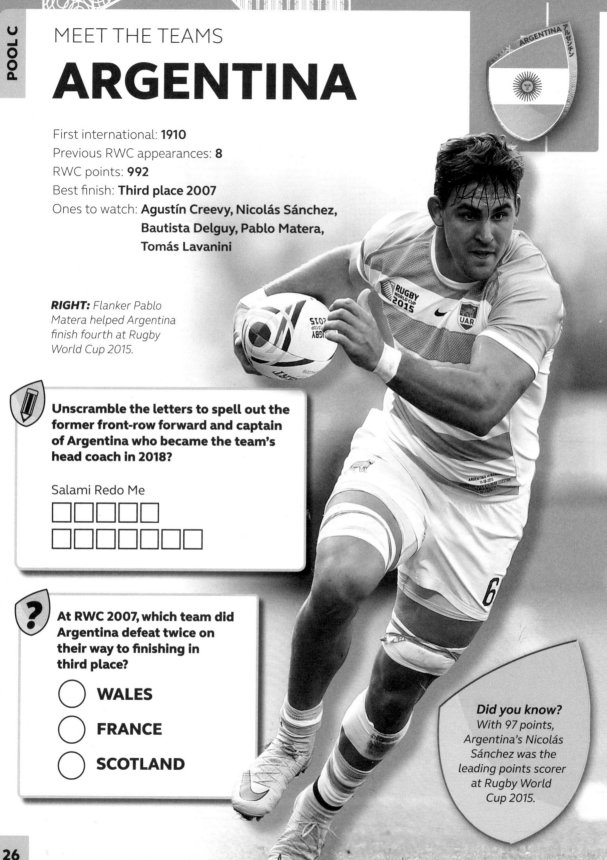

Unscramble the letters to spell out the former front-row forward and captain of Argentina who became the team's head coach in 2018?

Salami Redo Me

☐☐☐☐☐
☐☐☐☐☐☐☐

At RWC 2007, which team did Argentina defeat twice on their way to finishing in third place?

◯ **WALES**

◯ **FRANCE**

◯ **SCOTLAND**

Did you know?
With 97 points, Argentina's Nicolás Sánchez was the leading points scorer at Rugby World Cup 2015.

MEET THE TEAMS

USA

First international: **1912**
Previous RWC appearances: **7**
RWC points: **350**
Best finish: **Pool stage**
Ones to watch: **Joe Taufete'e,
Blaine Scully,
Samu Manoa,
AJ MacGinty**

LEFT: *USA number eight Samu Manoa catches the ball during a RWC 2015 match against Samoa.*

> **Did you know?**
> USA won both the 2017 and 2018 Americas Rugby Championships, defeating rivals Canada as well as Uruguay at both tournaments.

> **Did you know?**
> USA centre Juan Grobler was the only player at RWC 1999 to score a try against Australia.

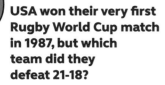

USA won their very first Rugby World Cup match in 1987, but which team did they defeat 21-18?

○ **ROMANIA**

○ **SAMOA**

○ **JAPAN**

MEET THE TEAMS

TONGA

First international: **1924**
Previous RWC appearances: **7**
RWC points: **405**
Best finish: **Pool stage**
Ones to watch: **Siale Piutau,
Sonatane Takulua,
Sitiveni Mafi**

LEFT: *Siale Piutau can play as a winger or a centre for Tonga and has scored two RWC tries.*

Did you know?
Tonga's youngest player was Elisi Busco Vunipola, who debuted in 1990 aged 17 years and 292 days. He appeared at both RWC 1995 and RWC 1999, and is the uncle of England stars Mako and Billy Vunipola.

 Which two of the following teams did Tonga beat at RWC 2011?

◯ **FRANCE**

◯ **CANADA**

◯ **JAPAN**

◯ **GEORGIA**

Tonga have played England in international matches just twice and Australia four times. In contrast, which team have they played 91 times?

◯ **FIJI**

◯ **NEW ZEALAND**

◯ **JAPAN**

MEET THE TEAMS

AUSTRALIA

First international: **1899**
Previous RWC appearances: **8**
RWC points: **1,645**
Best finish: **Champions 1991, 1999**
Ones to watch: **Kurtley Beale**
Bernard Foley,
Michael Hooper,
David Pocock,
Will Genia

RIGHT: *Will Genia fires a sharp pass during Australia's RWC 2015 semi-final win over Argentina.*

Did you know?
Australia have finished in the top four at six of the eight tournaments so far.

From these six players, can you pick the three who hold these Australian RWC records? Write their names in the spaces.

DAVID POCOCK	**DREW MITCHELL**
MAT ROGERS	**MICHAEL LYNAGH**
GEORGE GREGAN	**DAVID CAMPESE**

42: the most points scored in one RWC match

20: the most RWC matches played

14: the most RWC tries

MEET THE TEAMS

WALES

First international: **1881**
Previous RWC appearances: **8**
RWC points: **1,049**
Best finish: **Third 1987**
Ones to watch: **Taulupe Faletau, George North, Justin Tipuric, Leigh Halfpenny, Jonathan Davies**

RIGHT: Welsh winger George North thunders up the pitch against England at RWC 2015.

Wales' biggest Rugby World Cup win was a score of 81-7 against which team?

◯ **NAMIBIA**

◯ **SAMOA**

◯ **CANADA**

TRUE OR FALSE?

1) Wales beat Australia 22-21 in the third-place play-off at RWC 1987.

◯ *TRUE*   ◯ *FALSE*

2) George North is Wales' all-time leading Rugby World Cup try scorer.

◯ *TRUE*   ◯ *FALSE*

3) Sam Warburton captained Wales 49 times, more than any other player.

◯ *TRUE*   ◯ *FALSE*

Did you know?
Welsh second-row Huw Richards was the first player to be sent off at Rugby World Cup, in 1987.

MEET THE TEAMS

GEORGIA

First international: **1989**

Previous RWC appearances: **4**

RWC points: **197**

Best finish: **Pool stage**

Ones to watch: **Giorgi Nemsadze,
Merab Kvirikashvili,
Soso Matiashvili,
Vasil Lobzhanidze**

RIGHT: Georgia number eight
Lasha Lomidze powers through
a tackle at RWC 2015.

**Which one of these famous
England rugby players became
forwards coach of Georgia in 2018?**

○ **MARTIN JOHNSON**

○ **GRAHAM
ROWNTREE**

○ **LAWRENCE
DALLAGLIO**

Did you know?
*Georgia's all-time leading
try scorer is a forward,
the legendary Mamuka
Gorgodze, who
touched down
26 times.*

MEET THE TEAMS

FIJI

First international: **1924**
Previous RWC appearances: **7**
RWC points: **622**
Best finish: **Quarter-finals 1987, 2007**
Ones to watch: **Leone Nakarawa,**
Vereniki Goneva,
Semi Radradra,
Peceli Yato

LEFT: *Dynamic back-row Peceli Yato hopes to add to his tally of five international tries at RWC 2019.*

? **Which nation did Fiji travel to and defeat 21-14 in 2018?**

◯ **FRANCE**

◯ **SCOTLAND**

◯ **SOUTH AFRICA**

Did you know?
In Fiji's biggest ever RWC win, a 67-18 victory over Namibia in 1999, eight players scored tries and a ninth, Waisale Serevi, kicked 22 points.

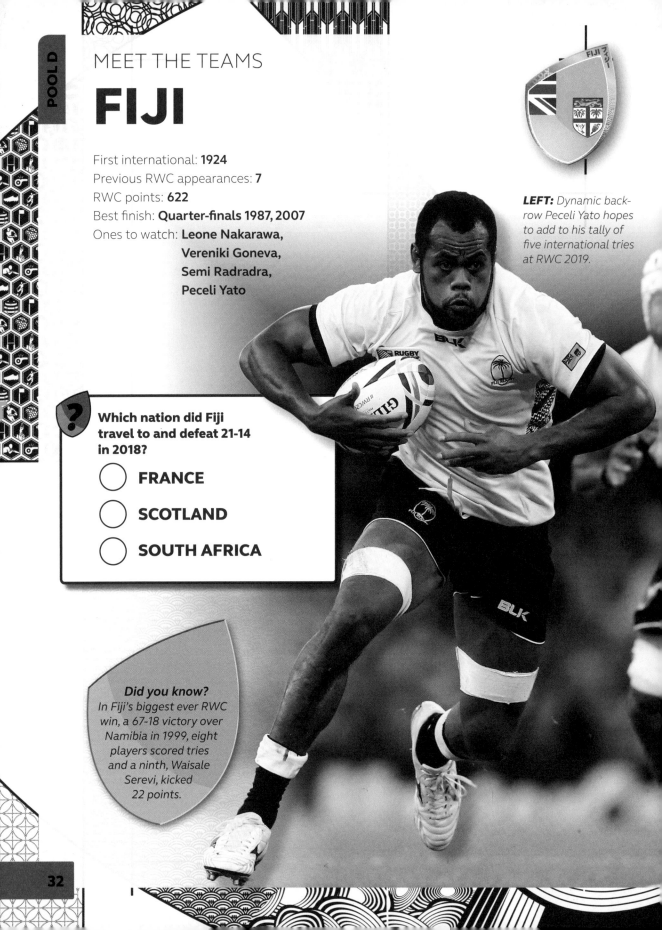

MEET THE TEAMS

URUGUAY

First international: **1948**
Previous RWC appearances: **3**
RWC points: **128**
Best finish: **Pool stage**
Ones to watch: **Leandro Leivas,**
Germán Kessler,
Felipe Berchesi,
Mario Sagario

LEFT: *Fly-half Felipe Berchesi is Uruguay's all-time leading scorer with 248 international points.*

At which Rugby World Cup did Uruguay score three tries to defeat Georgia 24-12?

○ **1999**

○ **2003**

○ **2015**

Did you know?
The Uruguay team are nicknamed Los Teros after the tero or southern lapwing bird that is found in the country's lakes and mountains.

Players and positions

For a rugby match, you need two teams of 15 players. Every player is expected to compete for the ball, pass, run, defend and tackle, but each has their own position, which may have extra responsibilities.

? **Uruguay's Diego Ormaechea is the oldest player to appear at Rugby World Cup. He was 40 years and 26 days old when he played against South Africa at RWC 1999, but in which position did he play?**

Did you know?
Twins Anthony and Saia Fainga'a played for Australia at RWC 2011. Anthony played in the backs as a centre, while Saia played among the forwards as a hooker.

POSITIONS, PLEASE!

A rugby team is set up in a scrum with the backs behind the scrum. Can you match each player to their correct playing position?

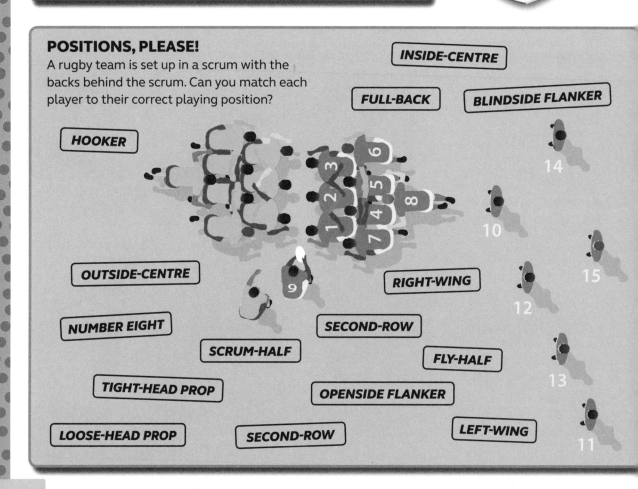

INSIDE-CENTRE

FULL-BACK

BLINDSIDE FLANKER

HOOKER

OUTSIDE-CENTRE

RIGHT-WING

NUMBER EIGHT

SECOND-ROW

SCRUM-HALF

FLY-HALF

TIGHT-HEAD PROP

OPENSIDE FLANKER

LOOSE-HEAD PROP

SECOND-ROW

LEFT-WING

RUGBY WORDSEARCH

There are 15 rugby words hidden inside this ball. Fourteen are written down or across, with one extra-hard entry running diagonally. Can you find them all?

- ○ TRY
- ○ PENALTY
- ○ SCRUM
- ○ LINEOUT
- ○ TACKLE
- ○ OFFSIDE
- ○ RUCK
- ○ MAUL
- ○ REFEREE
- ○ WINGER
- ○ CENTRE
- ○ BALL
- ○ PASS
- ○ TOUCH
- ○ BACKS

```
W D F F P N U G W N A H
G U F N A G U U I M A B
C V L K S F L Y N J C Z
G X I S S L P R G E R Y
S C E N T R E Q E E W V
O C M A J R Y P R Q P Y
R E F E R E E B B S E V
Z L I N E O U T A C N W
X L B O A I M N C B A Q
D P U F B I L Q K P L P
R J L F J T T S S I T I
I S U S K O A M X W Y F
P C U I R U C F A D V B
T M B D U C K O L U J A
R G B E C H L E O H L L
Y N L D K F E H S L O L
S C R U M S S S A Y S Q
S G K E Z O G M T C P U
```

1.
2.
3.
4.
5.
6.
7.
8.
9.
10.
11.
12.
13.
14.
15.

PLAYER WATCH

BACKS

A rugby team is split into eight forwards and seven backs. All players attack and defend, but backs are the players most expected to create and score tries. Here are some of world rugby's most exciting and successful match-winners.

STUART **HOGG**

Country: **Scotland**
Club: **Glasgow Warriors**
Born: **24 June, 1992**
Total caps: **67**
Total points: **107**

He's good at... racing through the tightest defences, using his searing pace to make breaks and score tries. The youngest player in the 2013 British and Irish Lions squad, Hogg was named Player of the Championship for the 2016 Six Nations for his exciting, attacking performances and great defence at full-back.

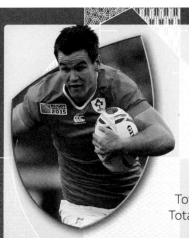

JOHNNY **SEXTON**

Country: **Ireland**
Club: **Leinster**
Born: **11 July, 1985**
Total caps: **83 (+6 Lions)**
Total points: **761 (+5 Lions)**

He's good at... controlling a match and kicking and passing to glory. With precise goal kicking and a knack of picking the right pass to keep the ball with his side, Sexton is considered the best fly-half in the northern hemisphere. He has won three Six Nations and four European Rugby Champions Cups.

BEAUDEN **BARRETT**

Country: **New Zealand**
Club: **Hurricanes**
Born: **27 May, 1991**
Total caps: **73**
Total points: **595**

He's good at... dominating matches for the All Blacks. The World Rugby Player of the Year in both 2016 and 2017 controls matches from fly-half and releases his team-mates with devastating passes or attacks himself. He has already scored 32 tries in international rugby and many more will surely follow.

OWEN **FARRELL**

Country: **England**
Club: **Saracens**
Born: **24 September, 1991**
Total caps: **70 (+4 Lions)**
Total points: **785 (+31 Lions)**

He's good at... goal kicking, defending robustly and leading a team. Farrell was just 17 years old when he debuted for Saracens and he became the club's all-time leading points scorer in 2017. For England, he plays at either fly-half or centre, where his reliable boot has won many matches for the side.

KURTLEY **BEALE**

Country: **Australia**
Club: **Waratahs**
Born: **6 January, 1989**
Total caps: **83**
Total points: **151**

He's good at... unlocking defences with a swift break or a sudden, creative pass. Beale mostly plays as a fly-half or centre, but he debuted for Australia in 2009 as a winger and has even played full-back. He helped the Waratahs win their first Super Rugby championship in 2014.

RIEKO
IOANE

Country: **New Zealand**
Club: **Blues**
Born: **18 March, 1997**
Total caps: **24**
Total points: **110**

He's good at... using his blistering pace to score tries, at an average of almost one every match. Ioane is a devastating runner in attack and one of the fastest backs in world rugby. His deceptive strength and fast footwork as well as his pace allow this former rugby sevens star to evade opponents and find space.

CONOR
MURRAY

Country: **Ireland**
Club: **Munster**
Born: **20 April, 1989**
Total caps: **72 (+5 Lions)**
Total points: **85 (+5 Lions)**

He's good at... bossing a scrum and taking chances. A tall scrum-half who defends strongly, Murray also seeks out tries with probing kicks, slick passes or darting runs. Forming a phenomenal partnership with Johnny Sexton, he scored a try and a penalty in Ireland's first ever win (40-29) over New Zealand in 2016.

WILLIE
LE ROUX

Country: **South Africa**
Club: **Wasps**
Born: **18 August, 1989**
Total caps: **53**
Total points: **60**

He's good at... gathering the ball and launching a blistering counter attack. Le Roux has played at fly-half and wing, but it's at full-back where he best uses his experience and vision to spot paths through defences. Le Roux is familiar with Japan, having played for Tokyo side Canon Eagles in 2015-17.

BEN
SMITH

Country: **New Zealand**
Clubs: **Highlanders, Otago**
Born: **1 June, 1986**
Total caps: **76**
Total points: **165**

He's good at... scoring or creating tries for others. The current vice-captain of the All Blacks, Smith plays wing or full-back and was a key part of the team that won RWC 2015. Man of the match in the semi-final against South Africa, Smith scored two tries in that tournament.

JONATHAN
DAVIES

Country: **Wales**
Club: **Scarlets**
Born: **5 April, 1988**
Total caps: **73 (+6 Lions)**
Total points: **75**

He's good at... linking play and making telling passes and offloads in close contests. Davies plays as a centre, where he brings out the best in his team-mates. In 2017, he returned from the drawn tour against New Zealand as the British and Irish Lions' player of the series.

WESLEY
FOFANA

Country: **France**
Club: **Clermont Auvergne**
Born: **20 January, 1988**
Total caps: **46**
Total points: **75**

He's good at... slicing through a defence with silky running, great ball handling and sudden changes of speed. Nicknamed 'The Cheetah' for his blistering pace, Fofana scored a try in each of his first four matches for France and has scored 15 international tries in total, despite missing many matches through injury.

FORWARDS

Forwards do the hard work in rugby, competing ferociously for the ball, securing it for their team and defending for all their worth when they lose it. Here are some of the world's most skilled and formidable forwards.

LEONE
NAKARAWA

Country: **Fiji**
Club: **Racing 92**
Born: **2 April, 1988**
Total caps: **53**
Total points: **60**

He's good at... playing like a forward and a back. Nakarawa is a powerful second-row with brilliant handling skills and he has surprising pace for a such a massive player! Nakarawa has scored tries at both the 2011 and 2015 tournaments and in 2018 he was voted European Player of the Year.

KIERAN
READ

Country: **New Zealand**
Club: **Crusaders**
Born: **26 October, 1985**
Total caps: **118**
Total points: **125**

He's good at... performing at his best, match after match. This number eight leads from the front, making lots of tackles and carrying the ball forward often. A two-time RWC winner, Read was made New Zealand captain in 2016 after Richie McCaw's retirement. He has scored 25 international tries, a phenomenal number for a forward.

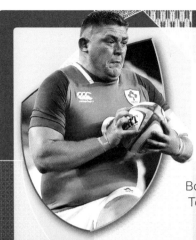

TADHG
FURLONG

Country: Ireland
Club: Leinster
Born: 14 November, 1992
Total caps: 33 (+3 Lions)
Total points: 5

He's good at... scrummaging and making powerful runs and tackles. Furlong is a tight-head prop with explosive power. He excels in sharp tackles and sudden bursts forward with the ball. He starred for Ireland in the 2018 Six Nations and on the British and Irish Lions tour of New Zealand in 2017.

MARO
ITOJE

Country: England
Club: Saracens
Born: 28 October, 1994
Total caps: 27 (+3 Lions)
Total points: 5

He's good at... getting involved all over the pitch. With great stamina and athleticism for a second-row, Itoje is often in the thick of the action, stealing lineout balls, tackling fiercely and making breaks with the ball. He debuted for England in 2016, when he also won the European Player of the Year award.

GUILHEM
GUIRADO

Country: France
Club: RC Toulon
Born: 17 June, 1986
Total caps: 68
Total points: 40

He's good at... tackling tirelessly and scrummaging relentlessly. A powerful presence in the French front row where he plays hooker, Guirado captained his side at Rugby World Cup 2015 and is keen to skipper France to glory at the 2019 tournament.

JAMES
RYAN

Country: **Ireland**
Club: **Leinster**
Born: **24 July, 1996**
Total caps: **17**
Total points: **5**

He's good at... winning the ball in lineouts and at rucks and carrying it forward with pace and power. Ryan is a young phenomenon who played for his country before his club. His 2017 debut for Ireland saw him score a try against USA, the start of a 21-match winning run for club and country that saw him be part of Ireland's triumphant 2018 Six Nations team.

DAVID
POCOCK

Country: **Australia**
Club: **Brumbies**
Born: **23 April, 1988**
Total caps: **77**
Total points: **45**

He's good at... making turnovers and stealing the ball. Pocock is seen as the best in the world at stealing possession when the ball is on the floor. Strong and with lightning reactions, Pocock was a key member of the Wallabies team that reached the final of Rugby World Cup 2015.

SIYA
KOLISI

Country: **South Africa**
Club: **Stormers**
Born: **16 June, 1991**
Total caps: **41**
Total points: **25**

He's good at... leading by example. Kolisi can play in any position in the back row, where he powers forward with the ball or tracks back to make tackles. South Africa's Players' Player of the Year in 2017, Kolisi was made captain of South Africa for their 2018 test series against England.

BILLY
VUNIPOLA

Country: **England**
Club: **Saracens**
Born: **3 November, 1992**
Total caps: **41**
Total points: **30**

He's good at... bulldozing his way through a defence. Surprisingly swift and sharp for such a big man, Vunipola is a powerful defender and a wrecking ball in attack, able to power through waves of defenders. Injuries have affected recent seasons, but when fit, he is one of the world's leading number eights.

ALUN
WYN JONES

Country: **Wales**
Club: **Ospreys**
Born: **19 September, 1985**
Total caps: **125 (+9 Lions)**
Total points: **45**

He's good at... dominating the lineout and securing the ball for his team. Jones debuted for Wales in 2006 and the veteran second-row rarely has a bad match. He is the first professional player to play nine consecutive British and Irish Lions test matches and helped drive Wales to the RWC 2011 semi-final.

MIKHEIL
NARIASHVILI

Country: **Georgia**
Club: **Montpellier**
Born: **25 May, 1990**
Total caps: **54**
Total points: **5**

He's good at... scrummaging, tackling hard and winning the ball in open play. Nariashvili is one of the best props in world rugby and a formidable opponent at scrum time. He has played his club rugby in France since 2010 and helped propel Georgia through an unbeaten 10-match qualification run for RWC 2015.

The pool stage

Keep track of the scores as the tournament progresses through the pool stage. Fill in the pool tables once all the matches are played.

POOL A

20 Sep – Tokyo Stadium
JAPAN [ ] – [ ] **RUSSIA**

22 Sep – International Stadium Yokohama
IRELAND [ ] – [ ] **SCOTLAND**

24 Sep – Kumagaya Rugby Stadium
RUSSIA [ ] – [ ] **SAMOA**

28 Sep – Shizuoka Stadium Ecopa
JAPAN [ ] – [ ] **IRELAND**

30 Sep – Kobe Misaki Stadium
SCOTLAND [ ] – [ ] **SAMOA**

3 Oct – Kobe Misaki Stadium
IRELAND [ ] – [ ] **RUSSIA**

5 Oct – City of Toyota Stadium
JAPAN [ ] – [ ] **SAMOA**

9 Oct – Shizuoka Stadium Ecopa
SCOTLAND [ ] – [ ] **RUSSIA**

12 Oct – Fukuoka Hakatanomori Stadium
IRELAND [ ] – [ ] **SAMOA**

13 Oct – International Stadium Yokohama
JAPAN [ ] – [ ] **SCOTLAND**

Team	W	D	L	Pts
1.				
2.				
3.				
4.				
5.				

POOL B

21 Sep – International Stadium Yokohama
N. ZEALAND [ ] – [ ] **S. AFRICA**

22 Sep – Hanazono Rugby Stadium
ITALY [ ] – [ ] **NAMIBIA**

26 Sep – Fukuoka Hakatanomori Stadium
ITALY [ ] – [ ] **CANADA**

28 Sep – City of Toyota Stadium
S. AFRICA [ ] – [ ] **NAMIBIA**

2 Oct – Oita Stadium
N. ZEALAND [ ] – [ ] **CANADA**

4 Oct – Shizuoka Stadium Ecopa
S. AFRICA [ ] – [ ] **ITALY**

6 Oct – Tokyo Stadium
N. ZEALAND [ ] – [ ] **NAMIBIA**

8 Oct – Kobe Misaki Stadium
S. AFRICA [ ] – [ ] **CANADA**

12 Oct – City of Toyota Stadium
N. ZEALAND [ ] – [ ] **ITALY**

13 Oct – Kamaishi Recovery Memorial Stadium
NAMIBIA [ ] – [ ] **CANADA**

Team	W	D	L	Pts
1.				
2.				
3.				
4.				
5.				

POOL A	POOL B	POOL C	POOL D
IRELAND	NEW ZEALAND	ENGLAND	AUSTRALIA
SCOTLAND	SOUTH AFRICA	FRANCE	WALES
JAPAN	ITALY	ARGENTINA	GEORGIA
RUSSIA	NAMIBIA	USA	FIJI
SAMOA	CANADA	TONGA	URUGUAY

POOL C

21 Sep – Tokyo Stadium
FRANCE ☐ – ☐ ARGENTINA

22 Sep – Sapporo Dome
ENGLAND ☐ – ☐ TONGA

26 Sep – Kobe Misaki Stadium
ENGLAND ☐ – ☐ USA

28 Sep – Hanazono Rugby Stadium
ARGENTINA ☐ – ☐ TONGA

2 Oct – Fukuoka Hakatanomori Stadium
FRANCE ☐ – ☐ USA

5 Oct – Tokyo Stadium
ENGLAND ☐ – ☐ ARGENTINA

6 Oct – Kumamoto Stadium
FRANCE ☐ – ☐ TONGA

9 Oct – Kumagaya Rugby Stadium
ARGENTINA ☐ – ☐ USA

12 Oct – International Stadium Yokohama
ENGLAND ☐ – ☐ FRANCE

13 Oct – Hanazono Rugby Stadium
USA ☐ – ☐ TONGA

Team	W	D	L	Pts
1.				
2.				
3.				
4.				
5.				

POOL D

21 Sep – Sapporo Dome
AUSTRALIA ☐ – ☐ FIJI

23 Sep – City of Toyota Stadium
WALES ☐ – ☐ GEORGIA

25 Sep – Kamaishi Recovery Memorial Stadium
FIJI ☐ – ☐ URUGUAY

29 Sep – Kumagaya Rugby Stadium
GEORGIA ☐ – ☐ URUGUAY

29 Sep – Tokyo Stadium
AUSTRALIA ☐ – ☐ WALES

3 Oct – Hanazono Rugby Stadium
GEORGIA ☐ – ☐ FIJI

5 Oct – Oita Stadium
AUSTRALIA ☐ – ☐ URUGUAY

9 Oct – Oita Stadium
WALES ☐ – ☐ FIJI

11 Oct – Shizuoka Stadium Ecopa
AUSTRALIA ☐ – ☐ GEORGIA

13 Oct – Kumamoto Stadium
WALES ☐ – ☐ URUGUAY

Team	W	D	L	Pts
1.				
2.				
3.				
4.				
5.				

Quarter-finals, semi-finals and the final

QUARTER-FINAL 1
19 October
OITA STADIUM
WINNER POOL C
v
RUNNER-UP POOL D

QUARTER-FINAL 2
19 October
TOKYO STADIUM
WINNER POOL B
v
RUNNER-UP POOL A

QUARTER-FINAL 3
20 October
OITA STADIUM
WINNER POOL D
v
RUNNER-UP POOL C

QUARTER-FINAL 4
20 October
TOKYO STADIUM
WINNER POOL A
v
RUNNER-UP POOL B

SEMI-FINAL 1
26 October
INTERNATIONAL STADIUM
YOKOHAMA
WINNER QUARTER-FINAL 1
v
WINNER QUARTER-FINAL 2
Final score
v
Try scorers

SEMI-FINAL 2
27 October
INTERNATIONAL STADIUM
YOKOHAMA
WINNER QUARTER-FINAL 3
v
WINNER QUARTER-FINAL 4
Final score
v
Try scorers

BRONZE FINAL
1 November
TOKYO STADIUM
LOSER SEMI-FINAL 1
v
LOSER SEMI-FINAL 2
Final score
v
Try scorers

THE FINAL

Fill in the details of the two teams that contest the final. Don't forget to add
'(C)' beside each team's captain and write down the points scorers.

2 November
INTERNATIONAL STADIUM YOKOHAMA

REFEREE

NAME

NAME

1.
1.

2.
2.

3.
3.

4.
4.

5.
5.

6.
6.

7.
7.

8.
8.

9.
9.

10.
10.

11.
11.

12.
12.

13.
13.

14.
14.

15.
15.

HALF-TIME SCORE

FINAL SCORE

TRY SCORERS

KICKS

MAN OF THE MATCH

Answers

PAGE 5: 271 tries

PAGE 6
- 15: Players in a team's starting line-up
- 40: Minutes per half
- 5: Number worn by a second-row
- 10: Minutes off the pitch for a player who is shown a yellow card
- 20: Additional minutes played when a match goes into extra-time
- 8: Number of players on each team who form a scrum

PAGE 7
Jonny Wilkinson: 277
Gavin Hastings: 227
Michael Lynagh: 195
Dan Carter: 191
Grant Fox: 170

PAGE 8
South Africa, Samoa and USA

PAGE 10: 1b; 2a; 3b

PAGE 11: 17 red cards

Spot the difference

PAGE 12: 1) 2003; 2) 1991; 3) 2015; 4) 1995

PAGE 13: 1999 and 2003

PAGE 14: 114 tries
Cian Healy and Garry Ringrose

PAGE 15
1987: 20-20 v France
1995: 89-0 v Ivory Coast
2007: 56-10 v Portugal
2015: 34-35 v Australia

PAGE 16: 711 points
Eddie Jones: 2015
Jamie Joseph: 2019
Shogo Mukai: 2003
John Kirwan: 2011

PAGE 17: 8 tries

PAGE 18: Wales

PAGE 19: Richie McCaw
Japan

PAGE 20: 8 tries
Argentina

PAGE 21: 1) True; 2) False; 3) True
Mauro Bergamasco

PAGE 22: Tunisia
Welwitschias

PAGE 23: Japan
Germany and Hong Kong

PAGE 24: Jamie George and Owen Farrell
111-13

PAGE 25: 1991 and 2007
Scotland

PAGE 26: Mario Ledesma
France

PAGE 27: Japan

PAGE 28: France and Japan
Fiji

PAGE 29
42 points in one RWC match:
Mat Rogers
20 RWC matches played:
George Gregan
14 RWC tries: Drew Mitchell

PAGE 30: Namibia
1) True; 2) False; 3) True

PAGE 31: Graham Rowntree

PAGE 32: France

PAGE 33: 2003

PAGE 34: Number eight

PAGES 34-35
1. Loose-head prop
2. Hooker
3. Tight-head prop
4. Second-row
5. Second-row
6. Blindside flanker (openside flanker in South Africa)
7. Openside flanker (blindside flanker in South Africa)
8. Number eight
9. Scrum-half
10. Fly-half
11. Left-wing
12. Inside-centre
13. Outside-centre
14. Right-wing
15. Full-back

PAGE 35

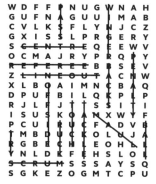